Anxiety

Strategies For Cognitive Behavioural Therapy, Emotional Intelligence, And Self-discipline Can Help You Clear Out Mental Clutter

(Strategies For Overcoming Anxiety, Curing Panic Disorders, Conquering Shyness, And Conquering Phobias)

DionisioMacia

TABLE OF CONTENT

Practical Exercises And Strategies 1

The Difficulties Encountered In Interpersonal Relationships Due To Anxious Attachment 10

The Efficacy Of Interpersonal Bonds In Promoting Healing 16

Minimizing Exposure And Sensitization To Stimuli 23

Unveiling Latent Stimuli 30

The Phenomenon Of Always Having The Last Word 62

What Factors Impede Or Hinder Your Progress Or Success? The Experience Of Panic, Worry, Stress, And Emotional Trauma 68

What Types Of Literature Do Those Classified As Billionaires And Millionaires Typically Engage With? 85

Strategies For Addressing Anxiety, Maladaptive Cognition, And Psychological Distress 118

Conclusion 144

Practical Exercises And Strategies

This section presents practical exercises and ideas for the application of Cognitive Behavioral Therapy (CBT) approaches in one's daily routine.

Cognitive restructuring involves a systematic approach to examining and altering negative beliefs by replacing them with more rational and balanced alternatives. This process entails step-by-step coaching to effectively question and reframe negative thoughts.

Exposure therapy is a therapeutic approach that involves systematically and gradually exposing individuals to anxiety-provoking circumstances in order to diminish fear and anxiety over a period of time. This method employs specific tactics for the effective implementation of the therapy.

Relaxation techniques refer to a variety of practices that aim to induce a state of calmness and reduce stress levels. These techniques encompass a range of methods, like as This study aims to investigate the efficacy of several relaxation exercises, including deep breathing, progressive muscle relaxation, and mindfulness, in the management of anxiety symptoms.

Homework Assignments: A Critical Examination This paper aims to elucidate the significance of homework assignments within the context of Cognitive Behavioral Therapy (CBT) and their role in reinforcing the abilities acquired during therapy sessions.

Constructing a Support System: This study aims to examine the significance of social support within the context of Cognitive Behavioral Therapy (CBT) and explore the potential benefits of integrating family members or friends in order to augment the therapeutic outcomes.

Upon completion of this , readers will acquire a thorough comprehension of the functioning of Cognitive

BehavioralTherapy (CBT), the capacity to recognize detrimental thought patterns that contribute to anxiety, and a collection of practical exercises and strategies to initiate the application of CBT techniques in their everyday lives. This implementation aims to foster enduring transformation and enhance emotional well-being.

This section provides an overview of practical exercises and tactics frequently employed in Cognitive-Behavioral Therapy (CBT) for the purpose of effectively managing anxiety. In order to facilitate a more comprehensive analysis, it is imperative to delve deeper into the content encapsulated within the five bullet points outlined in this particular section.

Distinguishing Between Typical Stress and Anxiety

It is imperative to acknowledge that experiencing occasional anxiety is a typical aspect of the human experience. Indeed, a certain degree of stress and worry might potentially provide advantageous outcomes by serving as a driving force and enhancing our performance. Nevertheless, in instances where the emotions of apprehension and trepidation reach an excessive level and begin to impede one's routine activities, it could potentially indicate the presence of an anxiety disorder.

An examination of the physiological and psychological ramifications of anxiety.

Anxiety exerts a significant impact not only on our psychological state but also manifests in several physiological ramifications. The presence of chronic stress and anxiety has been associated with adverse effects on the immune system, including its potential weakening. Additionally, those experiencing chronic stress and anxiety may be at an increased risk of developing high blood pressure and cardiovascular complications, such as heart difficulties. Furthermore, it is worth noting that this phenomenon can exert a significant influence on other aspects of our lives, including our interpersonal connections, professional achievements, and overall well-being.Root Causes of Anxiety

Anxiety is a prevalent mental health problem that impacts a significant number of individuals globally. It has the potential to present itself in diverse manifestations, such as generalized anxiety disorder, social anxiety disorder, and panic disorder. Although it may appear to be a daunting disease to live with, comprehending its underlying reasons will aid in comprehending this frequently incapacitating mental health concern.

The field of genetics plays a significant role in understanding the predisposition of individuals to certain traits or conditions.

There is a prevailing belief among researchers that anxiety disorders are influenced to a considerable extent by genetic factors. Research has indicated that persons who have a familial background of anxiety are at a higher risk of developing anxiety disorders themselves. This phenomenon can be attributed to the influence of specific genes, which may provide a predisposition towards heightened sensitivity to stress and the subsequent development of anxious behaviors.

However, possessing a genetic susceptibility does not guarantee the manifestation of an anxiety condition. The manifestation of [subject] is significantly influenced by environmental circumstances.

Kinesthetic-body intelligence refers to the cognitive capacity to effectively coordinate one's body and communicate through physical movement. This particular manifestation of intelligence pertains to the capacity to regulate not just one's own bodily motions, but also the aptitude to synchronize one's own bodily actions with those of others. An individual who possesses a pronounced kinaesthetic-body intelligence may exhibit exceptional aptitude in the creation of ballet, modern, or contemporary dance choreography.

Interpersonal intelligence refers to the cognitive capacity that involves comprehending and effectively engaging with others. The notion being discussed in this book bears a striking resemblance to emotional intelligence. However, according to Gardner's thesis, the capacity to comprehend the emotions of others is not correlated with the capacity to comprehend one's own emotions. In contrast, emotional intelligence integrates the capacity to comprehend both oneself and others into a unified construct. According to Gardner, the comprehension of others' emotions is distinct from and autonomous of comprehending one's own emotions.

Intrapersonal intelligence refers to an individual's capacity to comprehend and interpret their own emotions.

Individuals who possess well-developed intrapersonal intelligence typically exhibit a notable aptitude for introspection, self-assessment, and self-regulation. These individuals exhibit a high degree of introspection and frequently demonstrate exceptional sensitivity, a characteristic that can also lead to emotional distress. Individuals who experience heightened emotional sensitivity face the potential consequences of inviting external criticism and becoming vulnerable to personal attacks. In actuality, this particular manifestation of intellect holds significant importance and serves as an indicator of individual development. Sensitivity should not be regarded as a weakness, but rather as a strength. It is imperative to acknowledge that intellectual intelligence alone should not be deemed as the sole determinant of significance. The capacity to comprehend and empathize with emotions is equally vital in order to alleviate excessive rumination and ultimately embark upon a life of tranquility. Individuals who possess a high level of intrapersonal intelligence frequently exhibit exceptional aptitude in academic pursuits and artistic endeavors.

You have now obtained the most significant facts on Gardner's theory of intelligence. It is important to note, however, that this particular hypothesis is not the sole perspective on the existence of various forms of intelligence. In the subsequent part, an exposition will be provided regarding Sternberg's theory of intelligence.

The Difficulties Encountered In Interpersonal Relationships Due To Anxious Attachment

The presence of anxious attachment often gives rise to a distinct array of difficulties within interpersonal interactions. The aforementioned challenges can have an effect on both individuals with anxious attachment tendencies and their respective partners, leading to emotional turmoil and potential strain on their relationship. The following are several prevalent relationship difficulties that are commonly related with individuals exhibiting anxious attachment tendencies:

Persistent Need for Reassurance: Individuals exhibiting anxious attachment tendencies often exhibit an insatiable want for reassurance from their romantic partners. This phenomenon manifests as a recurring requirement for physical contact, vocal expressions of love and dedication, or continual reassurances that their spouse would not abandon them. In order to mitigate their inherent apprehension of being left alone, individuals seek reassurance.

The anxious attachment style is predominantly driven by a fear of abandonment. Minor alterations in a partner's conduct, such as their absence or delayed response to messages, can elicit significant levels of anxiety and unease in individuals. Individuals who encounter this particular apprehension may interpret ostensibly impartial actions as indicative of an imminent prospect of exclusion.

Jealousy and Insecurity: Within partnerships characterized by anxious attachment, the experience of jealousy frequently emerges as a prevalent issue. Individuals may experience unwarranted distress and see potential threats in their partner's interpersonal connections, even in the absence of any objective basis for concern.

Clinginess and possessiveness are commonly seen behavioral patterns among individuals with high degrees of anxiety in their interpersonal relationships. Individuals express concern that any form of separation or autonomy could potentially lead to the abandoning of their romantic relationship. Consequently, individuals exhibit an excessive need for attention, get overly engaged in their partner's endeavors, or encounter challenges in respecting their partner's need for personal space.

Challenges Associated with Establishing limits: Individuals who exhibit anxious attachment styles may encounter difficulties when it comes to establishing and maintaining appropriate limits. Individuals may encounter challenges in accurately perceiving instances where they impinge upon their partner's emotional autonomy or personal boundaries. The partner may experience a sense of being overwhelmed due to the infringement of personal boundaries resulting from these infractions.

Emotional Response: The emotional magnitude and volatility of interpersonal connections involving individuals with anxiety tendencies might be substantial. It is conceivable for individuals to experience rapid shifts between states of attachment and fondness, as well as periods of doubt and emotional distress. Both individuals involved in the partnership may experience fatigue due to the emotional fluctuations, making it challenging for them to manage these fluctuations consistently.

The impact of anxious attachment on relationship communication can be significant. Individuals who encounter difficulties in effectively conveying their thoughts often express their fears and uncertainties in manners that may potentially be perceived as assertive or controlling. This may lead to conflicts and misunderstandings.

The Urgency of Immediate Responses: Individuals who exhibit anxious attachment tendencies often exhibit a strong desire for timely reactions from their interpersonal connections. They may require consistent accessibility, whether it be through text messages, phone conversations, or face-to-face interactions. This expectation may impose a hardship and prove impractical for individuals who have many responsibilities, including their partner.

The Efficacy Of Interpersonal Bonds In Promoting Healing

It is inherent to human nature to possess a predisposition towards establishing connections with others. While solitude can have certain advantages, it is universally acknowledged that the presence of affectionate relationships is essential for individuals, as they offer solace, alleviate feelings of isolation, and foster a sense of empathy and comprehension. Engaging in recreational pursuits and spending meaningful moments with intimate relatives and companions who demonstrate genuine concern can serve as a comforting remedy for individuals experiencing worry.

To foster and maintain strong interpersonal connections, it is advisable to establish a consistent routine of engaging in social visits, participating in similar interests, and engaging in regular phone conversations. It is advisable to openly communicate about personal challenges with close individuals in order to receive support and reassurance, thereby acknowledging that one is not facing these difficulties in isolation. The perspective and suggestions offered by individuals can be of great value.

If individuals experience heightened levels of stress as a result of conflict or toxicity within specific relationships, it is advisable to establish and maintain appropriate boundaries in order to manage these interactions effectively. Preserve one's mental well-being while simultaneously upholding familial connections. It is advisable to cultivate social connections with those who possess positive attitudes and have a tendency to inspire and elevate one's spirits.

Seek out potential avenues for establishing fresh social connections by engaging in activities such as enrolling in educational courses, joining clubs or organizations, participating in volunteer initiatives, or attending networking gatherings. It is important to exercise caution in avoiding excessive commitments and to maintain a healthy equilibrium between social interactions and periods of solitude for rejuvenation.

Engaging in communal health-promoting activities, such as engaging in physical exercise as a group, preparing a shared meal, or attending live musical performances, serves to foster and sustain interpersonal connections, while simultaneously yielding positive effects on one's mental well-being by providing structure and enjoyment. Laughter is indeed a potent remedy, particularly in the presence of others with whom one shares a pleasant companionship.

Now, let us delve into more methods of utilizing the potential of social connection:

• Establish a consistent routine of video conferencing or arranging face-to-face meetings with intimate companions or family members.

• Engage in social activities such as meeting a companion for a coffee outing, taking a leisurely stroll, embarking on a shopping excursion, or partaking in a visit to a museum.

Engage in profound dialogues whereby you disclose concerns and provide reciprocal assistance.

Engage in the collaborative act of cooking and partake in communal dining, so transforming routine tasks into opportunities for social interaction.

One potential strategy for meeting individuals who share similar interests is to actively participate in a club or class centered around a hobby that brings personal enjoyment.

• Acquire a domesticated animal to provide regular companionship and emotional attachment.

• Participate in cost-free community events as a means of maintaining social engagement while avoiding excessive expenditure. • Foster a sense of camaraderie by engaging in shared physical activities such as attending the gym together or enrolling in dance classes.

• Engage in collective volunteerism to support a cause of mutual interest, such as participating in activities like walking shelter dogs.

Engage in recreational activities such as board games, card games, or video games that foster amusement and promote a spirit of friendly rivalry.

If an individual has children, they should arrange play dates and parents' night out events.

• It is advisable to reach out to friends in times of emotional distress or while seeking support and motivation.

One potential strategy to address the difficulties you are facing is to consider participating in a support group that is relevant to your specific concerns. This can be accomplished either through online platforms or by attending in-person meetings.

It is advisable to establish clear boundaries with relatives if their presence and interactions have a depleting rather than invigorating effect on one's well-being.

Minimizing Exposure And Sensitization To Stimuli

Having elucidated the aforementioned subtle stimuli, let us now delve into the strategies employed by superheroes to mitigate their adverse effects on one's state of being. Constructing a fortified structure serves as a means of safeguarding oneself against the tumultuous nature of emotional disturbances. Prior to delving into the effective ways for managing these triggers, it is essential to first understand the methods by which they can be identified.

Understanding and Identifying Personal Triggers

Please retrieve a magnifying glass as we embark on an exploration of the concept of recognition. Consider it as an exhilarating endeavor to decipher the clandestine communications emanating from one's own psyche.

Journaling serves as a means of connecting the dots between one's thoughts, likened to stars in the sky. Retrieve a notebook and expeditiously record your emotions while they are still vivid. The act can be likened to the collecting of fireflies in a jar, as it entails the preservation of instances characterized by emotional enlightenment. Through retrospective analysis of your records, it is possible to identify recurring trends that may serve as indicators of your triggers.

Mind maps are a visual tool used to organize and represent information. They are often used in educational settings to enhance learning and promote critical thinking. By utilizing a central idea or Mind maps can be likened to treasure maps, since they serve as navigational tools that assist individuals in navigating the intricate pathways of their own thoughts and ideas. Commence the cognitive process by initiating a primary stimulus, thereafter expanding into interconnected cognitions and affective experiences. The process might be likened to establishing connections between various points inside one's cognitive framework. This visual instrument facilitates the visualization of the interconnectedness of many triggers, so enabling a comprehensive understanding of the broader context.

occurrence tracking involves conceptualizing one's life as a chronological timeline, where each occurrence serves as a significant milestone. Engaging in the practice of monitoring one's daily behaviors and emotions might be likened to assuming the role of a personal time traveler. When experiencing a certain emotional state, it can be beneficial to reflect upon preceding events that occurred within the same day or week. Similar to the investigative methods employed by Sherlock Holmes, one may perhaps identify the underlying cause by retracing their actions and scrutinizing the concealed elements.

Self-observation involves the mental exercise of envisioning oneself at a movie theater, where one assumes the role of an observer, attentively watching their thoughts projected onto the expansive screen. Self-observation might be likened to assuming the roles of both the actor and the director simultaneously. When an abrupt change in one's emotional state is seen, it is advisable to take a momentary break and engage in introspection by posing the question: "What transpired to elicit this alteration?" The act might be likened to momentarily halting the mental projection of one's thoughts in order to discern the specific scene that serves as the catalyst.

● Therapeutic guidance: Similar to how explorers seek the assistance of guides, individuals might seek the support of professionals for therapeutic purposes. Therapists and counselors might be likened to seasoned navigators adept at navigating the complex terrain of triggers. Professional individuals possess the capability to assist in untangling intricate cognitive processes and illuminating areas of limited awareness. Having a co-pilot accompanying one on their emotional trip can be likened to the experience being described.

One aspect that can be beneficial for individuals is the availability of group assistance. Consider the scenario when one is engaged in the process of deciphering a substantial puzzle, whereby each individual piece represents a distinct viewpoint or perspective. Group assistance might be likened to the presence of puzzle partners who actively contribute their perspectives and thoughts. Engaging in a support group or engaging in conversations with people who possess a comprehensive understanding of your situation might offer novel perspectives on the factors that elicit emotional responses. Engaging in collaboration can be likened to the process of collectively piecing together the intricate puzzle that is one's emotional landscape.

The process of identifying one's triggers might be likened to the intricate assembly of a puzzle. The revelation of each clue serves to progressively enhance one's comprehension of their emotional map. As the principal investigator, these tactics serve as essential tools in your investigative arsenal. By employing these strategies, individuals are actively engaging in the process of understanding and managing their triggers, hence enhancing their ability to effectively navigate challenging situations.

Unveiling Latent Stimuli

The identification of concealed triggers that initiate the manifestation of anxiety is a pivotal stage in the progression towards a state of tranquility. Anxiety, a commonly experienced psychological phenomenon, is influenced by a range of internal and external factors. In the present , we will embark on a quest to locate these triggers and get further knowledge regarding their impact on us.

Identifying Individual Anxiety Stimuli

Individuals may experience varying anxiety triggers, which is a common occurrence. The initial stage in effectively managing anxiety involves the identification of the specific triggers that elicit such a response within an individual's life. These triggers encompass a wide range of factors, including specific situations, environments, individuals, as well as cognitive processes and recollections. By acknowledging these triggers, individuals empower themselves to respond in a proactive manner.

The anxiety causes might be conceptualized as individual pieces of a jigsaw puzzle. A more comprehensive understanding of one's anxiety context can be attained through the process of uncovering and gathering relevant information. Maintain a journal wherein one records instances of heightened anxiety, including temporal details, contextual activities, social companionship, and cogitations that transpired. Over time, discernible patterns will emerge, guiding individuals towards effective strategies for managing anxiety.

The Impact of Environmental Factors on Anxiety

The impact of the environment on mental health is substantial.

The surrounding environment might occasionally serve as a catalyst for anxiety. Feelings of unease can be intensified by various factors such as excessive noise, disorganized surroundings, a high-pressure occupation, or even a chaotic living environment. This section will examine the potential impact of one's environment on anxiety levels and offer practical approaches for creating a tranquil situation.

It is important to consider that environmental triggers exhibit significant individual variability. The perception of relaxation might vary among individuals, since what may induce a state of calmness for one person might elicit feelings of anguish in another. The creation of environments conducive to tranquility can be achieved through heightened self-awareness of one's personal preferences and sensitivities.

The Significance of Perceptions and Cognitive Processes

The emotional state of individuals can be influenced by their views. Anxiety frequently arises from cognitive distortions characterized by inaccurate or irrational thought patterns. The situation can be likened to a narrator recounting an impending catastrophe. This section will examine the intricate relationship between cognitive processes and anxiety, with a particular focus on the role of maladaptive thought patterns as significant precipitators.

The efficacy of worry can be diminished by the acquisition of skills in confronting and reframing these cognitive constructs. We will offer a range of activities and strategies aimed at assisting individuals in gaining mastery over their thoughts and effectively reshaping them into narratives that are more positive in nature.

Trauma is a psychological and emotional response to an event or experience that is deeply distressing or disturbing. It can result from a

The enduring impact of trauma, characterized by the lingering reverberations of distressing previous events, exerts a profound influence on the individuals who have undergone such experiences. Anxiety may be attributed as both a significant catalyst and instigator, resulting in lasting impressions on an individual's psyche and reconfiguring their emotional terrain. In order to comprehend the intricate correlation between trauma and anxiety, it is imperative to delve into the profound realms of human distress and adaptability.

Trauma has the potential to present itself in various manifestations, encompassing physical, emotional, and psychological dimensions.

The origins of this phenomenon can be traced back to instances of childhood maltreatment, traumatic accidents, experiences in military warfare, or other profoundly distressing occurrences. When an individual experiences trauma, it has the potential to profoundly disrupt their perception of safety and trust, resulting in enduring emotional wounds that may last for an extended period, possibly even throughout their lifetime.

One of the significant manners in which trauma impacts mental well-being is by serving as a catalyst for the development of anxiety disorders. The trauma experience has the potential to reconfigure the neural pathways in the brain, thereby preparing it for an elevated state of alertness. Anxiety can be understood as an adaptive mechanism, serving as a means for the mind to maintain a constant state of vigilance in order to detect potential threats.

Furthermore, it is important to note that trauma has the potential to act as a catalyst for the development of anxiety in the current context. It is possible for a seemingly unrelated event or condition to unintentionally evoke memories or sensations linked to the traumatic episode. This phenomenon has the potential to induce a condition of heightened anxiety or extreme terror in the affected individual, commonly known as post-traumatic stress disorder (PTSD).

The association between trauma and anxiety extends beyond a solitary temporal occurrence and manifests over an extended duration. Individuals who have experienced trauma may develop persistent anxiety, characterized by a continual apprehension and concern around the potential reoccurrence of catastrophic events. Nightmares, flashbacks, and hyper vigilance emerge as undesirable companions during the process of recovery. However, among the distressing terrain of trauma and anxiety, the resilient human spirit persists. Numerous individuals who have experienced trauma exhibit the resilience to address their previous experiences, actively pursue therapeutic interventions, and implement various coping mechanisms in order to restore a semblance of personal agency. The journey towards achieving wellness is frequently challenging, however it serves as a testament to the remarkable capacity for resilience inherent in the human condition.

Empathy and support are key components within the context of trauma and anxiety narratives. Recognizing the correlation between trauma and the development of anxiety, as well as acknowledging the intricate and non-linear nature of the healing process, cultivates a caring atmosphere conducive to the well-being of survivors.

This statement serves as a poignant reminder that even in the most profound depths of the human condition, there exists the potential for individuals to exhibit resilience, undergo a process of rehabilitation, and ultimately embrace hope.

Methods for acquiring the skill of meditation

The practice of meditation for beginners is sometimes perceived as more straightforward than commonly believed. By adhering to the approach outlined below, specifically designed for individuals who have attempted meditation numerous times without achieving desired results, one can effectively engage in this practice.

Tips for Beginners to Start Practicing Meditation

The introductory phase of meditation often encompasses a plethora of advice and lesser-known information. However, it is feasible to impart uncomplicated techniques for enhancing concentration and organization, thereby facilitating the initiation of meditation practice and yielding prompt outcomes. This initial progress serves as an incentive to delve deeper into the practice, elevating one's proficiency and augmenting the level of concentration attained.

One crucial consideration to have in mind when engaging in meditation is the establishment of a clear and defined objective. By consistently recalling this objective at the commencement of each meditation session, individuals can enhance their ability to maintain focus and remain committed to the practice, particularly in the context of beginner-level meditation.

It is important to determine the specific amount of time you intend to allocate for practice and establish a consistent timetable to ensure regular adherence, irrespective of factors such as travel, inclement weather, or personal health. Similar to engaging in regular physical exercise, the practice of meditation need to be incorporated into one's daily routine and initiated in a progressive manner.

Another crucial aspect to consider is maintaining a comfortable posture. The primary focus of meditation for novice practitioners pertains to the phenomenon whereby individuals frequently discontinue their engagement in this practice due to the experience of discomfort or agony when meditating. This phenomenon occurs due to the misconception that one must exclusively assume the lotus position while meditation. However, it is important to note that meditation can be practiced while seated on a chair, reclining on a bed, or even positioned on the floor.

If individuals continue to experience a lack of security when engaging in independent meditation, they may consider exploring guided meditation films specifically designed for beginners, which can be found on the online platform, YouTube. They will provide invaluable advice that will enhance your sense of security and self-assurance, crucial aspects for individuals embarking on their meditation journey and seeking encouragement to progress with the practice.

By engaging in this practice, individuals can enhance their knowledge, acquire novel methodologies and positions, gain valuable insights on breathing and concentration, and establish a deeper connection not only with their inner selves but also with the surrounding environment, which is crucial in the context of meditation.

Key Points from the

Rather than perceiving one's passions solely as enjoyable leisure activities, it is advisable to consider them as significant endeavors that might assume a more profound significance in one's life.

The alignment between one's passions and their natural talents or learned skills can be observed. It is important not to underestimate the value of one's past life experiences, as they can provide valuable insights into one's distinctive qualities.

The acquisition of expertise in any domain necessitates a substantial amount of patience and a steadfast commitment to achieving the highest standards of performance. However, this is not a matter that should instill fear. It is advisable to adopt a broad perspective while simultaneously focusing on the minutiae and purposefully considering each decision pertaining to one's life.

It is anticipated that individuals may experience feelings of discomfort and worrisome thoughts when embarking onto unfamiliar endeavors. This behavior might be interpreted as a manifestation of courage and a willingness to embrace the inherent risks associated with personal development and the acquisition of knowledge. Avoid becoming immobilized by overthinking or fixating on the opinions and judgments of others. It is imperative to reflect upon the significance of residing in Ikigai and then engage in proactive measures.

The user has effectively accomplished the initial segment of the book. Thus far, the acquired knowledge pertains to the historical roots and semantic significance of Ikigai, with an examination of certain fallacious interpretations associated with this philosophical notion. The user has acquired knowledge regarding the three drivers of Ikigai, their application in the pursuit of purpose, and the prevalent fear that may impede progress. The subsequent section of the book will now be explored, whereby the emphasis will be placed upon personal growth and the discernment of one's intrinsic worth.

Traumatic or adverse experiences

When a someone undergoes a negative or traumatic event, they may experience acute discomfort in the immediate aftermath. However, it is important to note that the impact of such an encounter might extend beyond its immediate occurrence, leaving a lasting impression on the individual involved. Several commonly reported situations that occur in the school years have been associated with individuals who experience social anxiety. Bullying serves as a prominent illustration, along with other instances that isolate individuals as peculiar, slightly divergent, and socially unacceptable, which collectively contribute to the development of social anxiety over the course of one's lifetime.

Post-traumatic stress disorder (PTSD) frequently arises as a prevalent outcome of acute traumatic events, hence exacerbating pre-existing social anxiety problem. The persistent recurrence of negative memories through flashbacks hinders the ability to approach social situations with objectivity, since it perpetuates the dominance of negative thoughts in one's head.

The Challenges Posed by Existence

When engaging in conversations with individuals diagnosed with social anxiety disorder, a significant portion of them tend to report a lifelong presence of the condition, whereas others indicate that its onset occurred during adolescence or early adulthood. Adolescents and young individuals encounter numerous challenges, particularly in the realm of social interactions, as they embark on the journey towards independence and strive to create their adult identity within societal expectations.

Public schools provide several possibilities for individuals to encounter socially challenging circumstances and events. Effectively navigating these circumstances to prevent the development of Social Anxiety Disorder (SAD) necessitates substantial assistance and open dialogue. Overcoming these hurdles poses significant difficulty, and the behavioral patterns established by these young individuals may exert long-term effects on their future prospects, rendering certain aspects of life challenging to navigate. A significant number of high school students encounter challenges in adapting to the college environment, as they grapple with the need to assimilate and invest considerable effort in impressing their peers in terms of both physical appearance and intellectual prowess.

The contemporary burdens

There exist two distinct forms of stress that are prone to influence an individual's anxiety levels: major relocations that result in severed connections with colleagues, friends, and/or family; and significant alterations that impact an individual's interpersonal relationships, such as a job transition. These demands necessitate rapid adaptation to a novel circumstance and require a substantial amount of energy, which is likely to be scarce.

Engaging in situations that include meeting unfamiliar individuals and cultivating novel connections can be initially anxiety-inducing, as one endeavors to assess the dynamics and acquaint oneself with the other party, all while striving to present oneself in the most favorable light. The magnitude of the pressure to make a favorable impression and the apprehension of experiencing failure can give rise to considerable levels of anxiety. The development of confidence is a necessary process that often coincides with the emergence of past vulnerabilities.

The term "technology" refers to the application of scientific knowledge and tools for practical purposes.

The prevalence of social anxiety disorder, classified as one among several anxiety disorders, is increasing. There is an increasing prevalence of individuals who appear to be experiencing a sense of disconnection and encountering difficulties in navigating their interactions within contemporary society. The prevalence of depression has exhibited a notable upward trend, and this association between anxiety disorders and depression is not limited to a singular manifestation. It has been shown that a significant proportion, specifically 50%, of individuals who receive a diagnosis of depression also have symptoms of anxiety, and conversely, a comparable percentage of individuals diagnosed with anxiety also exhibit symptoms of depression. Antidepressants rank as the second most often prescribed medication in the United States, but the incidence of suicide exhibits an upward trend annually.

The examination of anxiety disorders has encompassed the examination of several factors such as heredity, hormone imbalance, and environmental situations. However, an additional pivotal aspect that warrants consideration is the impact of technology. The experience of alone is significant among individuals afflicted with Seasonal Affective Disorder (SAD) and depression. Technological advancements have provided us with the capacity to enhance our connectivity while concurrently experiencing heightened feelings of loneliness. However, one may question the feasibility of this phenomenon. Let us examine the case study of Greenland.

Currently, Greenland exhibits one of the most elevated suicide rates globally. However, this phenomenon did not commence until little rural communities began to experience depopulation due to the mass migration of individuals seeking employment and educational opportunities in the capital city. It is commonly assumed that those residing in larger communities would experience reduced feelings of loneliness and depression compared to those living in smaller villages with a population of only 50 inhabitants. Nevertheless, as proximity grew, Greenland encountered a decline in its communal cohesion. The presence of other individuals does not exclusively determine an individual's experience of anxiety or despair. It is widely acknowledged that individuals can have profound feelings of loneliness even while surrounded by a collective of individuals. Human beings possess an inherent social nature, whereby the absence of a supportive society can engender a sense of purposelessness in one's existence.

The impact of technology in the United States can be likened to the consequences of centralized jobs and education in Greenland. The advent of digital communication has provided individuals with unprecedented access to engage in conversations with a vast number of others, reaching into the hundreds or even millions. However, it is noteworthy that these encounters often fail to delve beyond superficial exchanges and establish meaningful relationships. The prevalence of screen-based interactions has led to a decline in our ability to engage in face-to-face communication, resulting in heightened levels of anxiety in social settings when our actions are observed by others rather than being limited to textual exchanges on digital platforms.

Technology is a highly advantageous instrument; yet, rather of employing it in a manner akin to a carpenter's utilization of a saw, we tend to allow ourselves to be controlled by it. Has anyone ever encountered a carpenter utilizing a saw? No individual. The aforementioned approach is not effective in yielding the desired outcomes. However, individuals in contemporary society are heavily reliant on screens, allowing them to exert significant influence over several facets of our existence. If a someone discovers that they are allocating a greater amount of time engaging with screens as opposed to engaging in face-to-face interactions with individuals in the physical realm, it is plausible that they have identified one of the contributing factors to their social anxiety disorder (SAD).

If individuals discover that they are facing this issue, it may be necessary for them to acquire the skill of regulating their usage of electronic devices. One potential solution is to configure your smartphone to implement a data usage restriction, so restricting the reception of data beyond a specified threshold. Alternatively, it may be advisable to discontinue smartphone usage entirely and revert to a basic cellular device until such time that you feel more capable of managing its usage more effectively.

It is possible to observe that the social circle one maintains may not effectively foster a sense of community. It is possible that one may perceive a persistent sense of scrutiny due to the presence of judgmental individuals within their social circle. The sense of uneasiness may be attributed to the persistent nagging one receives when engaging in social activities with friends. It may be opportune to seek for alternative companions. As previously said, a multitude of support groups are available to individuals experiencing Seasonal Affective Disorder (SAD), which can serve as a valuable community fostering a sense of purpose.

In contemporary times, there is a tendency to dismiss traditions and religious beliefs due to their perceived antiquity and lack of scientific validity. Nevertheless, the significance of one's cultural history and traditions may surpass one's initial perception. Cicero, in one of his writings, expressed the notion that perpetual ignorance of historical events prior to one's own lifetime is akin to a state of perpetual childhood. The significance of human life is contingent upon its integration into the historical narrative through ancestral records. In the absence of a compass, our navigational abilities are limited, rendering us akin to vessels adrift on the vast expanse of the ocean, subject to the whims of whichever wave happens to seize hold of us. The experience of residing in such a manner engenders a significant level of worry.

The Phenomenon Of Always Having The Last Word

The ego possesses the ability to transform every aspect of an individual's identity into a self-centered theatrical production. If an individual realizes that they frequently engage in self-centered conversations without showing interest in their partner's experiences, it can be inferred that they possess a significant degree of egocentrism. The ego has a significant role in impeding our ability to achieve complete peace and joy. It represents the cognitive mechanism by which the mind exercises control. It will also generate circumstances in your account that are non-existent. If one realizes that they possess an incessant desire to assert their final opinion in all matters, it is imperative for them to retrospectively examine the underlying cause of this compulsion. Do you have the belief that you possess superior qualities compared to others or do you perceive yourself as being of lesser quality? Do you have a deficiency in self-assurance and, as a result, feel compelled to prove your worth despite the challenges? The ego might lead individuals to mask their perception of mediocrity by exaggerating their own abilities. If frequent conflicts arise between oneself and their partner, it is likely that one's ego plays a significant role in exacerbating these disputes. Is it important for one to experience such emotions within the context of their relationship?

It is necessary to periodically engage in introspection and evaluate one's interpersonal connections. The desire is to be able to recognize instances in which one is at fault or committing errors. Examine one's behaviors and recognize instances in which they are motivated by ego. In order to cultivate a robust and harmonious connection with one's spouse, it is imperative to relinquish one's ego.

If an individual possesses a substantial sense of self-importance or their affection is characterized by excessive self-centeredness, what course of action must be undertaken?

The narcissistic individual's feeling of self-worth is closely intertwined with their constant need to be accurate. In this manner, persons who are unable to let go of their ego engage in unrestricted behavior and discourse, perpetually maintaining an unwavering belief in their own infallibility. Regrettably, this may come at the cost of numerous other factors. The consistent demonstration of infallibility might potentially jeopardize one's interpersonal connections, including relationships with colleagues, supervisors, family members, relatives, and particularly significant others. In due course, it becomes imperative to recognize that the spurious sense of self-worth derived from egoistic pursuits and the pursuit of being right fails to surpass authentic well-being.

Cultivating self-loyalty and engaging in mindfulness practices will facilitate the recognition that one cannot invariably possess absolute correctness in every situation. There may arise circumstances in which one commits an error, possesses a misguided mindset, or finds oneself in complete opposition to the correct perspective.

Acknowledging one's errors can be challenging, although possessing the ability to concede when mistaken can yield a sense of liberation. By assuming accountability for one's actions and judgments, it becomes evident that the responsibility for the outcome will ultimately lie with the individual.

There is no necessity to surpass or outperform anyone in one's immediate vicinity. The pressure to conform to societal expectations can frequently have detrimental effects on one's well-being. A strong sense of self-importance fosters the belief in one's superiority over others. It is akin to acknowledging the fallibility of one's own judgments and recognizing that one cannot always be infallible. It should be understood that there is no absolute requirement to surpass others in terms of performance or abilities. The level of competitiveness exhibited by individuals is not conducive to maintaining a state of good health.

Invariably, there will exist those that surpass one's abilities, physical attractiveness, intelligence, agility, and financial resources. Irrespective of one's age, this phenomenon may persist indefinitely. The sooner one comprehends the inherent impossibility and undesirability of striving for superiority over others, the sooner one can begin to mend and enhance their interpersonal connections.

What Factors Impede Or Hinder Your Progress Or Success? The Experience Of Panic, Worry, Stress, And Emotional Trauma

Congratulations, you have successfully reached the last week of your challenge. This subject matter is quite captivating, isn't it? At this point, one should experience a sense of heightened invincibility. This week will prioritize the most ambitious objectives to instill motivation and sustain momentum.

Below is a compilation of essential tasks that should be consistently performed on a daily basis:

It is recommended to engage in daily reading of the extensively expanded list to enhance comprehension and retention.

- Documenting levels of anxiety and tracking progress.

- Write up your triggers and assumed triggers. • Write out what you are grateful for.

Day Twenty-Two

Find your weekly objective for today and do what you have always done and build a game plan of actions to undertake in order to complete it. It is advisable to complete one of the aforementioned chores within the present day. After that, go to a store and get a hula hoop. Engage in the activity of returning to your place of residence and engaging in the physical exercise of hula hooping for a duration of 15 minutes without interruption. Afterward, relax by taking a hot bath with either Epsom salts or aromatherapy.

Day Twenty-Three

As you are writing out what you perceive to be your assumed triggers and actual triggers this week, pick an assumed trigger to tackle today. Make a plan as for how to approach it and go. Refer to breathing techniques and positive mental activities if you are overwhelmed. Whether you were successful or not, go home and perform some simple stretches. Relax afterward by calling up a buddy to talk to either about your progress or your failing attempt. They could offer some helpful advice to give you a greater shot of success if they happen to understand you well.

Day Twenty-Four

Today, instead of picking an assumed trigger, pick a trigger that you are fully confident about. Make your game plan, and go. Just go straight through your nervousness and that will be the only way to overcome it. Remember to refer to the breathing exercises and good mental exercises. After your attempt, go home and dance to 5 entertaining songs giving yourself one-minute rests in between songs. Afterward, discover a hilarious movie or videos on the internet that will make you chuckle.

Day Twenty-Five

Today, select a movie showing at a theater that you would most likely love and go see it alone. You may feel strange being by yourself when there are couples on dates or groups of friends and relatives, but this activity will only help you learn to be okay with yourself and alone yourself. Sometime today, try to go swimming or perform yoga for at least 30 minutes. Help yourself unwind by sitting outside for 30 minutes also.

Day Twenty-Six

Just like yesterday, conduct an activity alone. Go shopping alone. Even if your budget won't support it, go to at least 5 stores and look at their stuff. While you are shopping, try going around the whole entire mall. Depending on how big or small your mall may be, this is where you receive your exercise for the day. When you go home, rest from the overstimulation you may have felt in the mall by listening to relaxing music for 30 minutes.

Neuroplasticity

In the preceding two decades, study has found that the mind has an astonishing degree of neuroplasticity, which signifies a capability to change its structures and remodel its ways of responding. Indeed, even sections of the brain that were long regarded impossible to change in adults are equipped for being transformed, disclosing that the mind actually has an incredible ability to change (Pascual-Leone et al. 2005). For instance, individuals whose thoughts are harmed by strokes can be trained to utilize various pieces of the cerebrum to move their arms (Taub et al. 2006). In particular settings, circuits in the mind that are utilized for vision can build up the ability to react to sound in only a couple of days (Pascual-Leone and Hamilton 2001).

New connection in the brain regularly produce in startlingly basic manners: exercise has been suggested to accelerate far reaching development in synapses (Cotman and Berchtold 2002). In some research, even contemplating taking specific activities, such as tossing a ball or playing a tune on the piano, might produce alterations in the zone of the cerebrum that controls those advancements (Pascual-Leone et al. 2005). Furthermore, certain drugs advance development and modifications in circuits of the cerebrum (Drew and Hen 2007), particularly when combined with psycho-treatment. Additionally, psychotherapy alone has been appeared to cause alterations (Linden 2006), lowering activation in one zone and enhancing it in others.

Unmistakably, the cerebrum isn't permanent and unchangeable, as many people once imagined. The complete resolution of the circuits inside the cerebrum is not just determined by genetic factors, but is also influenced by an individual's experiences and cognitive and behavioral patterns. It is possible to modify the functioning of the brain to elicit unforeseen responses, irrespective of an individual's age. While there exist certain limitations, it is noteworthy to acknowledge the remarkable capacity for flexibility and potential for change inside the human brain, including its ability to modify its predisposition towards generating excessive levels of worry.

We will provide guidance in harnessing the principles of neuroplasticity, coupled with a comprehensive understanding of the functioning of the cortex and amygdala pathways, in order to facilitate long-lasting transformations inside the human brain. One can employ this information to modify the neural architecture of the brain in order to enhance its resilience to stress, rather than exacerbating it.

It is imperative to commence this section by assuring that all the information we provide on the mind is valuable and practical, aiming to elucidate the underlying causes of anxiety and facilitate an understanding of how to modify one's mindset in order to mitigate the experience of worry. This exposition does not aim to provide comprehensive and specialized depictions of all the intricate neurological processes involved. Instead, it offers a concise and foundational elucidation of anxiety in the human mind, with the intention of facilitating comprehension of the efficacy of specific approaches in managing anxiety.

while individuals lack an understanding of the underlying causes of their anxiety, they may find themselves unprepared while attempting to initiate its transformation. Anxiety is generated by the cerebrum and is contingent upon the contributions of specific regions inside the mind. Considering the complicated and interrelated nature of the cerebrum, a significant portion of its functioning remains enigmatic. There exist alternative strategies that can be employed to address these specific worries, hence enhancing one's effectiveness in managing or mitigating the experienced worry.

The act of observing one's thoughts

In the contemporary global context, individuals are compelled to engage in many actions. In addition to effectively managing daily pressures, it is imperative to cultivate constructive habits that serve as a deterrent against excessive concern and negative thinking. The demanding surroundings and the fast-paced nature of our daily lives frequently inundate our minds with a multitude of thoughts and distractions. Frequently, there arises a juncture wherein our cognitive faculties are unable to cease their ruminative processes. Individuals may experience a state of cognitive overload, resulting in a disorganized mental state. Does this statement really reflect your personal characteristics and traits? If affirmative, then it can be inferred that your cognitive faculties are signaling a state of surrender and may necessitate a process of organizing and streamlining.

Similar to the practice of frequently allocating time to organize and tidy one's office and living space, the mind also necessitates decluttering. This will ensure the creation of additional capacity to enhance optimal performance. Nonetheless, the task is not as straightforward as it may initially appear, as one is unable to directly perceive the contents of another individual's thoughts. Consequently, the cleaning procedure will deviate from the customary decluttering practices to which you have become accustomed. Inquiring as to the process by which one may effectively eliminate superfluous thoughts from their cognitive faculties. The present discussion will be centered on providing a response to the aforementioned inquiry, so facilitating comprehension of the importance associated with the act of clearing one's thoughts.

The factors contributing to the presence of mental clutter.

In a typical scenario, when engaging in the process of cleaning a residential or professional environment, one would commence by discerning the objects that contribute to disorderliness. Similarly, prior to engaging in the process of mental decluttering, it is imperative to commence by discerning the underlying factors contributing to the presence of mental clutter. The significance of engaging in this practice lies in its ability to ensure the efficient management of clutter over an extended period of time. One will have a heightened awareness of the various elements that contribute to mental congestion and make conscious efforts to mitigate their impact.

The subsequent factors are frequently attributed to the occurrence of cognitive overload.

The concept of overwhelm refers to a state of being excessively burdened or inundated with tasks

If an individual experiences a state of being overwhelmed, it is likely to result in cognitive disarray. Consequently, individuals may find it challenging to devise a rational approach for addressing their concerns. This phenomenon leads to the accumulation of disorganized and excessive objects or materials. Fortunately, one can surmount this challenge by recognizing the reality that it is not feasible to manage all tasks simultaneously. It is advisable to decompose your activities into smaller, yet feasible sub-tasks. It is advisable to address each of these matters individually and sequentially. By the conclusion of the day, one will come to the realization that a substantial amount of tasks have been successfully completed, without experiencing a sense of being excessively burdened.

The phenomenon of over-commitment refers to the state in which an individual takes on more responsibilities

Engaging in a commitment to complete certain tasks listed on one's agenda is a commendable endeavor. However, in situations where one is unable to decline additional duties, it indicates an excessive level of commitment. Attempting to manage an excessive number of tasks will inevitably result in feelings of dissatisfaction. This is due to the potentiality of encountering difficulties in successfully executing the task. The acquisition of the ability to decline requests or opportunities is a fundamental characteristic necessary for leading a highly efficient and fruitful existence. The act of declining should not be perceived negatively, since it signifies a commitment to effectively allocate one's resources towards manageable tasks. It is advisable to refrain from overextending one's commitments and assuming responsibilities above one's capacity.

The emotion of fear is a common human experience that is characterized by a feeling of unease

Individuals who experience apprehension towards relinquishing past events are prone to exert mental pressure. The tendency to retain possessions and ideas frequently engulfs individuals. Rather than engaging in constructive tasks, the mind tends to persistently dwell on past events. The present content can be characterized as excessive and disorganized. What are the reasons for subjecting oneself to such torment when it is possible to acquire the skill of relinquishing attachment?

What Types Of Literature Do Those Classified As Billionaires And Millionaires Typically Engage With?

Through extensive research and careful selection, I have identified a collection of books that serve as a solid foundation for cultivating intellectual prowess, enhancing cognitive abilities, and fostering critical thinking skills.

The Psychological Influence of Persuasion: Which Offers Insights into Human Behavioral Influence. This text discusses the six rules of influence and highlights the significant impact of influence, as well as strategies to avoid succumbing to its effects.

Prominent Quotation: "An individual who possesses exceptional negotiation skills is characterized by an initial stance that is sufficiently inflated, enabling a sequence of compromises that would ultimately lead to a favorable and conclusive proposal from the opposing party, without being perceived as inherently unreasonable from the outset."

Endorsed by Charlie Munger and the author.

In the book titled "How to Win Friends and Influence People" authored by Dale Carnegie, the author provides guidance on effective interpersonal communication and strategies for building and maintaining positive relationships. This book has the potential to strengthen an individual's cognitive processes, leadership abilities, and behavioral patterns via the cultivation of empathy and true respect for others. Additionally, it can significantly improve one's communication skills, leading to a more profound and effective mode of expression. As a result, the transformative impact of this book on an individual's life is undeniable.

Prominent Quotations: The abilities in question exhibit enhanced growth when subjected to positive reinforcement, whereas they may face scrutiny when subjected to criticism.

Endorsed by Warren Buffet and a multitude of 15 million individuals, including me.

In his renowned work "Think & Grow Rich," Napoleon Hill explores the profound impact of one's beliefs on individual life experiences, while also delving into the concept of mastermind groups. Millionaires also highly endorse the establishment of a mastermind group, which can be defined as a collective of individuals collaboratively pursuing their respective objectives.

Prominent Quotation: Prior to achieving success, individuals are bound to encounter numerous instances of short setbacks and conceivably experience failure. When faced with defeat, it is often the most effortless and rational course of action for an individual to abandon their pursuits. This is precisely the behavior exhibited by the majority of males. The author was informed by over five hundred highly accomplished individuals, who are widely regarded as some of the most successful persons in this nation's history, that their greatest achievements occurred immediately after experiencing defeat.

Endorsed by Tony Hartl and the author.

The Bible offers individuals genuine purpose in life, serving as a source of inspiration and hope.

Prominent Quotation: The Bible encompasses a vast collection of verses and quotes that offer guidance and support in all aspects of life, including financial matters, physical well-being, motivation, and sagacity. Among them, a particular verse that resonates with me is Isaiah 61: 1-3.

The presence of the Divine Being, known as the Sovereign Lord, is bestowed upon me, since I have been consecrated by the Lord to announce favorable tidings to individuals experiencing economic hardship.

He has been assigned the task of binding the wounds of those who are emotionally distressed, declaring liberation for those who are imprisoned, and offering release from the state of darkness for those who are held captive. Additionally, he is to proclaim the period of time when the Lord's favor is bestowed and the day when God's retribution will be enacted. His purpose is to bring comfort to all who are grieving and to provide for those who are sorrowful in the city of Zion. Ultimately, his mission is to grant them a symbol of honor and beauty in place of their current state of desolation, to offer them a sense of joy instead of mourning, and to clothe them with a spirit of praise rather than despair.

These individuals shall be referred to as "oaks of righteousness," symbolizing their righteousness and strength. They are divinely planted by the Lord, intended to showcase His magnificence and glory.

The book titled "Awaken the Giant Within: How to Take Immediate Control of Your Mental, Emotional, Physical, and Financial Destiny" contains a notable quote.Take pleasure in the process of making decisions. It is crucial to acknowledge that at any given moment, a decision made by an individual has the potential to significantly alter the trajectory of their life indefinitely. This alteration may be triggered by seemingly inconsequential events such as standing behind a particular individual in a queue or sitting next to a specific person on an airplane, as well as engaging in or receiving a particular phone call. Furthermore, the consumption of specific media, such as watching a particular movie, reading a particular book, or turning a specific page, may also serve as the catalyst that unlocks a series of favorable circumstances, leading to the realization of long-awaited aspirations. To cultivate a passionate life, it is necessary to adopt an attitude of expectation.

Through extensive research and careful selection, I have identified a collection of books that serve as a solid foundation for cultivating intellectual prowess, enhancing cognitive abilities, and fostering critical thinking skills.

The Psychological Influence of Persuasion: Which Offers Insights into Human Behavioral Influence. This text discusses the six rules of influence and highlights the significant impact of influence, as well as strategies to avoid succumbing to its effects.

Prominent Quotation: "An individual who possesses exceptional negotiation skills is characterized by an initial stance that is sufficiently inflated, enabling a sequence of compromises that would ultimately lead to a favorable and conclusive proposal from the opposing party, without being perceived as inherently unreasonable from the outset."

Endorsed by Charlie Munger and the author.

In the book titled "How to Win Friends and Influence People" authored by Dale Carnegie, the author provides guidance on effective interpersonal communication and strategies for building and maintaining positive relationships. This book has the potential to strengthen an individual's cognitive processes, leadership abilities, and behavioral patterns via the cultivation of empathy and true respect for others. Additionally, it can significantly improve one's communication skills, leading to a more profound and effective mode of expression. As a result, the transformative impact of this book on an individual's life is undeniable.

Prominent Quotations: The abilities in question exhibit enhanced growth when subjected to positive reinforcement, whereas they may face scrutiny when subjected to criticism.

Endorsed by Warren Buffet and a multitude of 15 million individuals, including me.

In his renowned work "Think & Grow Rich," Napoleon Hill explores the profound impact of one's beliefs on individual life experiences, while also delving into the concept of mastermind groups. Millionaires also highly endorse the establishment of a mastermind group, which can be defined as a collective of individuals collaboratively pursuing their respective objectives.

Prominent Quotation: Prior to achieving success, individuals are bound to encounter numerous instances of short setbacks and conceivably experience failure. When faced with defeat, it is often the most effortless and rational course of action for an individual to abandon their pursuits. This is precisely the behavior exhibited by the majority of males. The author was informed by over five hundred highly accomplished individuals, who are widely regarded as some of the most successful persons in this nation's history, that their greatest achievements occurred immediately after experiencing defeat.

Endorsed by Tony Hartl and the author.

The Bible offers individuals genuine purpose in life, serving as a source of inspiration and hope.

Prominent Quotation: The Bible encompasses a vast collection of verses and quotes that offer guidance and support in all aspects of life, including financial matters, physical well-being, motivation, and sagacity. Among them, a particular verse that resonates with me is Isaiah 61: 1-3.

The presence of the Divine Being, known as the Sovereign Lord, is bestowed upon me, since I have been consecrated by the Lord to announce favorable tidings to individuals experiencing economic hardship.

He has been assigned the task of binding the wounds of those who are emotionally distressed, declaring liberation for those who are imprisoned, and offering release from the state of darkness for those who are held captive. Additionally, he is to proclaim the period of time when the Lord's favor is bestowed and the day when God's retribution will be enacted. His purpose is to bring comfort to all who are grieving and to provide for those who are sorrowful in the city of Zion. Ultimately, his mission is to grant them a symbol of honor and beauty in place of their current state of desolation, to offer them a sense of joy instead of mourning, and to clothe them with a spirit of praise rather than despair.

These individuals shall be referred to as "oaks of righteousness," symbolizing their righteousness and strength. They are divinely planted by the Lord, intended to showcase His magnificence and glory.

The book titled "Awaken the Giant Within: How to Take Immediate Control of Your Mental, Emotional, Physical, and Financial Destiny" contains a notable quote.Take pleasure in the process of making decisions. It is crucial to acknowledge that at any given moment, a decision made by an individual has the potential to significantly alter the trajectory of their life indefinitely. This alteration may be triggered by seemingly inconsequential events such as standing behind a particular individual in a queue or sitting next to a specific person on an airplane, as well as engaging in or receiving a particular phone call. Furthermore, the consumption of specific media, such as watching a particular movie, reading a particular book, or turning a specific page, may also serve as the catalyst that unlocks a series of favorable circumstances, leading to the realization of long-awaited aspirations. To cultivate a passionate life, it is necessary to adopt an attitude of expectation.

The familial context

The development and recovery of individuals with borderline personality disorder are influenced by the immediate family environment.

The concept of self-complexity refers to the extent to which individuals perceive themselves as having

Individuals diagnosed with borderline personality disorder exhibit a multitude of features and undergo a diverse range of emotional experiences simultaneously. The presence of self-complexity poses significant challenges for psychiatrists in their efforts to provide effective treatment for those diagnosed with borderline personality disorder. Patients afflicted with this disorder have an internal struggle characterized by a multitude of paradoxes, rendering it challenging to assist them in recognizing the necessity of maintaining a consistent emotional trajectory.

The phenomenon of suppressing thoughts

Suppression, a frequently seen defense technique among individuals diagnosed with borderline personality disorder, entails a deliberate endeavor to evade specific thoughts that may engender feelings of vulnerability. The act of suppressing thoughts has been observed to lead to increased secrecy and resistance to treatment in individuals diagnosed with borderline personality disorder.

Borderline personality disorder (BPD) is a personality disorder that exhibits conspicuous symptoms, although it presents significant challenges in terms of treatment due to patients' self-awareness and resistance to change. However, it remains feasible to facilitate their recovery via consistent therapy and the exercise of patience.

17. Conduct an olfactory assessment of your partner's garment.

There exist numerous strategies for managing stress. However, a recent and remarkable discovery has been made. It is noteworthy to mention that the statement in question is supported by scientific evidence, which may elicit surprise among individuals. According to a study conducted at the University of British Columbia and published in the Journal of Personality and Social Psychology, it was discovered that the olfactory perception of one's romantic partner's scent has the potential to reduce levels of stress.

The study conducted by the researchers revealed that women experience a heightened state of relaxation upon exposure to the scent of their partners. On the other hand, the exposure to unfamiliar individuals' odor elicits a rise in the secretion of cortisol, a hormone associated with stress.

The conclusion was derived from a sample of 96 heterosexual couples who took part in the study. During the experiment, male subjects were given specific instructions to wear a T-shirt for a duration of 24 hours, refraining from the use of any body-scented products, such as deodorant. In addition, limitations were imposed on the consumption of cigarettes and specific food items that have the potential to alter one's olfactory perception.

The male participants' T-shirts were assigned to female participants by the researchers. Subsequently, the female participants proceed to olfactorily evaluate the shirt that has been presented to them. The individuals were not provided with information regarding the specific shirt that belongs to their spouse.

Additionally, women were subjected to a series of stress tests. The experiment encompassed a simulated employment interview and a cognitive arithmetic task. Subsequently, the investigators quantified the concentration of cortisol present in the participants' saliva. The results indicate that female participants who were exposed to the olfactory stimuli of their romantic partner exhibited a reduced concentration of stress-related hormones in comparison to those who were exposed to the scent of an unfamiliar individual's garment.

What are recommended strategies for managing stress? Engage in olfactory analysis of your partner's garment. However, what are the underlying factors that contribute to its functionality? Why does being exposed to the scent of a stranger induce stress in individuals?

The authors postulate that the initial apprehension towards unfamiliar individuals in our early evolutionary history may have triggered this hormonal response. Children exhibit fear towards unfamiliar individuals, particularly those of the male gender. The researchers posit that the outcome of the study may have been influenced by a similar sense of fear.

Nevertheless, the investigation solely concentrated on the female demographic. The existence of the same finding among men remains uncertain. Is it advisable for males to engage in the act of smelling their partner's shirt as a means of alleviating stress? This question merits further scientific investigation.

However, this discovery carries various implications. Couples may possess a significant advantage in this regard. This could potentially provide assistance to individuals who experience physical separation due to the demands of their professional occupations.

The contemporary professional landscape may exhibit heightened levels of demand compared to previous eras. Certain individuals may have a professional obligation to travel to different urban centers or even various regions across the globe in order to fulfill their occupational responsibilities. The act of leaving or retaining a well-worn shirt or cloth belonging to a cherished individual can provide significant assistance.

20. Alter the atmosphere

Light plays a crucial role in the sustenance of life. All living organisms depend on the intricate workings of this remarkable natural phenomenon. Light plays a crucial role in facilitating the growth and development of various organisms, ranging from plants to animals of diverse species. The influence of lighting on humans extends beyond its physical effects, encompassing emotional dimensions as well.

A recent study has yielded a noteworthy discovery. The emotional response can be influenced by a specific color of lighting. In a study conducted by Jesus Minguillon et al., it was observed that exposure to blue light resulted in a more rapid reduction in stress levels compared to conventional white light sources.

The study's conclusion was derived from the participation of 12 individuals. The participants were intentionally subjected to stress and subsequently divided into two groups of equal size. During the subsequent phase of the investigation, the participants were subsequently subjected to a relaxation session within the chromotherapy room.

One cohort was subjected to white light, whereas the other cohort was subjected to blue light. Upon the conclusion of the study, the researchers determined that the participants who were allocated to the blue light condition exhibited a higher level of relaxation compared to the individuals in the alternative group.

The study authors provided an explanation stating that blue lighting has been found to expedite the relaxation process following exposure to stress, as compared to conventional white lighting.

The relaxation time exhibited a reduction of approximately three-fold, with values of 1.1 minutes and 3.5 minutes, respectively.

Additionally, a convergence time of 3.5-5 minutes was observed, at which point the previously observed advantage of blur lighting ceased to exist.

Nevertheless, this particular study did not mark the inaugural scientific inquiry conducted to comprehend the influence of lighting on human emotions.

The authors referenced comparable studies that examined the impact of wall color on learning environments. Specifically, one study demonstrated that pale colors induced greater relaxation compared to vivid colors, and that heart rate decreased when exposed to short-wavelength colors such as violet, blue, and green, as opposed to longer-wavelength colors like yellow and red.

Moreover, several authors have effectively addressed individuals with behavior disorders through the manipulation of their emotional states, such as inducing mental tranquility, using color lighting techniques.

An example of the successful application of pink light was observed in the context of reducing aggression among incarcerated individuals.

Additionally, another method utilizing color-based lighting, specifically blue light, has been employed in the treatment of disruptive behavior disorders.

The discovery possesses utility not solely for professionals, but also for the general populace. The implementation of a basic blue lighting system within our residential environment has the potential to mitigate levels of stress experienced by individuals.

A Comparative Analysis of Healthy and Unhealthy Relationships

In order to acquire knowledge on the transformation of unhealthy relationships into healthy ones, it is imperative to develop a comprehensive understanding of the characteristics and dynamics inherent in a healthy relationship. While varying types of relationships exhibit distinct criteria for measuring their level of health, they generally adhere to a comparable set of guidelines. This subwill primarily center on the dynamics of a healthy romantic relationship in order to streamline the discussion.

In order to cultivate a thriving romantic relationship, it is imperative for the couple to possess three essential components: effective communication, well-defined boundaries, and constructive relationship-enhancing strategies.

The establishment of honest, open, and safe communication is imperative in fostering a mutually beneficial and sustainable relationship. The initial phase of constructing a relationship necessitates a comprehensive understanding and mutual acknowledgement of each individual's respective needs and expectations. It is imperative that both individuals involved possess a shared understanding and alignment in their perspectives. In order for two individuals to achieve mutual understanding, it is imperative that they engage in continuous and effective communication. The majority of healthy relationships adhere to the following five components:

When a relationship is characterized as healthy, individuals involved in the relationship exhibit a willingness to openly communicate about any issues or concerns, rather than suppressing them internally.

Respect is a fundamental aspect of a healthy relationship, wherein both individuals hold a deep regard for one another's desires and emotions. Mutual communication is established to inform one another of their respective endeavors to prioritize their own welfare. The establishment of mutual respect is a fundamental component in cultivating a robust and thriving interpersonal connection.

In healthy relationships, it is common for arguments or disagreements to arise, necessitating the acquisition of the skill of compromise. This skill becomes crucial when two individuals find themselves in disagreement over a particular matter. Individuals engaged in healthy relationships employ effective conflict resolution strategies, employing compromises as a means to mutually satisfy both parties involved.

- Assertion: Healthy relationships are characterized by mutual support and the absence of derogatory behavior. It is imperative for individuals engaged in a romantic partnership to consistently provide each other with encouragement and reassurance. It is imperative to communicate with one another regarding the need for assistance.

Privacy is an essential component of maintaining healthy relationships, as it allows for the necessary space and personal time that each individual requires. The mere fact that two individuals are in a romantic partnership does not necessitate their constant physical proximity or the complete sharing of all aspects of their lives.

Presented below is a compilation of scenarios that manifest maladaptive behaviors within the context of a romantic relationship.

One's romantic partner exhibits feelings of jealousy or anger in response to interactions with individuals other than oneself.

The individual with whom you are in a relationship frequently engages in phone calls and text messages to ascertain the individuals in your company and your current whereabouts.

One's partner may exhibit physical aggression or engage in verbal aggression.

Your partner engages in derogatory behavior, which includes belittling, emotional manipulation, and verbal abuse.

The individual with whom you are in a relationship employs tactics such as intimidation, negotiation, or coercion in order to compel you to engage in actions that you do not desire to undertake.

The individual with whom you are in a relationship exhibits behavior that includes making threats to cause harm to your personal belongings, domesticated animals, acquaintances, and relatives.

The individual with whom you are in a relationship exercises authority over your actions and provides instructions regarding your conduct and obligations.

It is recognized that the individuals in question do not possess the desired qualities of a significant other, yet there exists a belief that their attributes can be altered.

The individual in question is chosen as a companion due to the belief that this choice is preferable to solitude.

Physical intimacy is a fundamental aspect that holds significant importance within a relationship.

The individual in question possesses exclusive authority in determining their actions and destinations.

There is a frequent occurrence of arguments among the individuals in question.

Individuals consistently engage in the act of ridiculing or belittling one's personhood.

One experiences a sense of embarrassment when engaging in public activities with one's romantic partner.

The individual in question lacks the availability to allocate time towards other individuals or activities.

When an individual is in the company of their peers, they may experience instances where they are subjected to humiliation or being disregarded.

The discussion of contraception or safe sex is not permissible.

● They engage in derogatory discourse about your family. ● They assert authority over your clothing choices and dictate your actions.

They disseminate false and negative information about an individual.

Strategies For Addressing Anxiety, Maladaptive Cognition, And Psychological Distress

There exist multiple strategies for combating anxiety, negative thinking, and stress.

Comprehending Your Cognitive Approach

The initial phase in the process involves taking action to transform the often pessimistic sentiments commonly experienced. It is vital to possess a comprehensive understanding of one's cognitive processes. Below are several cognitive frameworks that can assist in enhancing one's thinking abilities:

Individuals who hold the belief that failure in one aspect equates to failure in all aspects might be classified as polarised or black and white thinkers.

Individuals who possess the ability to discern the perceptions others hold of them and the underlying motivations behind their behaviour, even in the absence of explicit communication, might be characterised as individuals prone to making hasty inferences.

Individuals who consistently anticipate negative outcomes in various situations, regardless of the circumstances, might be classified as catastrophizing thinkers. This particular cognitive individual consistently poses the inquiry: "what if?"

The capacity to identify cognitive distortions

Upon successfully recognising one's cognitive style, individuals can subsequently ascertain whether it constitutes a cognitive distortion or not. The aforementioned mental distortions exemplify many types as outlined in the initial stage. These cognitive distortions encompass catastrophizing, engaging in excessively negative forecasting, and engaging in dichotomous thinking.

The capacity to identify and acknowledge the cognitive process of rumination.

Rumination refers to a cognitive process characterised by the repetitive and intrusive fixation on negative thoughts, emotions, or experiences. A profound or contemplative reflection on a subject matter. In general, individuals see a notable decline in their problem-solving abilities when engaging in rumination. Hence, it is imperative for individuals to acknowledge and refrain from encountering this particular phase in the process of problem-solving.

If one has difficulty in avoiding rumination, the optimal course of action during episodes of rumination is to acknowledge the presence of specific thoughts, acknowledge their potential fallibility, and subsequently permit them to dissipate naturally within one's own cognitive processes, rather than attempting to suppress them.

Dealing with Criticism

Criticism is an inevitable facet of human existence. Conversely, insufficient management of the aforementioned situation may result in unwarranted concerns. Consequently, it is imperative for individuals to have the skill of effectively managing and responding to criticism. Cognitive Behavioural Therapy (CBT) has the potential to facilitate the acquisition of essential skills necessary for effectively managing criticism. In the context of a therapeutic session, it is advisable to carefully evaluate the constructive nature of blame before determining its potential utility or dismissal. It is imperative to consistently support one's beliefs with evidence in order to make informed decisions grounded in factual information.

Acquire Proficiency in the Practise of Mindfulness

Mindfulness refers to a cognitive state that is attained through the deliberate concentration of one's attention on the current moment, accompanied by a serene recognition and acceptance of one's emotions, thoughts, and physical sensations. The primary association lies in the practise of meditation.

Acquiring proficiency in the practise of mindfulness can facilitate the regulation of one's cognitive processes and affective states. This phenomenon occurs because to the instructional nature of art, which encourages individuals to perceive their ideas and emotions as entities that drift by, affording them the ability to halt, examine, or allow them to continue on their course. This topic will be addressed progressively during our discussion.

The Capacity for Self-Compassionate Internal Dialogue Regarding Imperfections and Errors

The significance of engaging in self-critical inner dialogue in response to personal imperfections has been found to be negligible. This phenomenon arises mostly due to its tendency to induce rumination, subsequently resulting in the generation of ambiguous problem-solving strategies. Conversely, empirical studies have demonstrated that engaging in self-directed, composed discourse can enhance one's self-motivation and elicit a heightened sense of well-being.

The act of preventing or inhibiting the occurrence of thought stopping.

Thought stopping and mindfulness are diametrically opposed concepts. This discipline involves actively monitoring one's thoughts for any negative content and exerting deliberate effort to eradicate them. One issue associated with this particular behaviour is that the act of actively suppressing these thoughts may inadvertently lead to their heightened occurrence during the process of problem-solving. Hence, refraining from such ideas and adopting a practise of mindfulness is a far more advantageous approach.

Comprehending the Cognitive Reflection Diary

What is the definition of thinking journals? There exist various tools that can be employed to modify negative thoughts. The significance of these cognitive journals lies in their ability to assist individuals in recognising and assessing their negative cognitive patterns, so facilitating a deeper comprehension of the impact of their beliefs on their emotional state. The utilisation of diaries is vital within a cognitive behavioural treatment regimen and is a necessary component for the documentation of one's ideas. There exist additional practical considerations that need be addressed prior to reaching a definitive conclusion.

This book contains actionable steps and strategies on how to release yourself from the perpetual chains of anxiety.

Evolution has primed us humans to respond in a certain manner when faced with uncertainty and this is being anxious. The reason for this is simple; when we become anxious, our bodies respond by going into a 'fight or flight' mode, which prepares us to deal with the imminent threat. While our bodies are wired to go back to a state of normalcy after a few moments of being anxious i.e. after the uncertainty has ceased, there are times when we may not go back to the normalcy that we should go back to. This may happen even when the uncertainty is truly nothing that would warrant us to respond by having consistently high levels of fight and flight chemicals within our body.

Obviously, this is bound to bring about lots of problems especially because of the high levels of body chemicals that are usually secreted during a fight and flight response. This can result to chronic anxiety levels, which can have severe behavioral, physiological and psychological effects all of which point to you not achieving your full potential.

Do you find yourself more often anxious than calm? Has this affected your life such that you are unable to enjoy every single moment as it unfolds because you are always anxious about something? If you are tired of this and want to do something about it, this book will help. It will simplify the process of overcoming anxiety by breaking it down into 5 simple steps that are easy to follow.

The autobiographical memory network is used to process information that is related to one's self. A person will really only find that their autobiographic memory network turns on once they become preoccupied with thoughts surrounding one's self. This can include being able to recall personal memories or opportunities for self-reflection. The main components of this network include the areas that makeup the prefrontal cortex, which sits at the front of the brain. The main areas of the prefrontal cortex are the hippocampus, the posterior cingulate cortex, and the parietal regions that are central for a person's mental imagery.

The cognitive control network and the autobiographical memory network are thought to have a bit of a strained relationship. This is mainly due to the fact that the autobiographic memory network only sets in once a person becomes consumed with thoughts about themselves. Those thoughts then lead to the cognitive control network shutting off because the brain is no longer focused on being task-oriented. As a result, the person will find that there is a reduction in their ability to finish any task they were supposed to have completed. That is actually why daydreaming can be such a hindrance to a person's work.

Conversely, there are cases where the autobiographic memory network is not in use because the cognitive control network is in the process of gaining the necessary attention of the brain in order to complete a current task. It is in these types of cases that people use the phrase that a person is "losing themselves" in their work because they are so absorbed with the task at hand that they are not paying attention to what their body and mind need.

When the cognitive control network and the autobiographic memory network to not work correctly, that is what can lead to what is known as mood disorders. Just like how there are two main networks in the brain, there are two main types of mood disorders. The first one is depressive disorders, which are characterized by a person having their mood be persistently down. The other primary mood disorder is bipolar disorder, which there occurs when a person expresses extreme highs and equally extreme lows. The highs that a person has during bipolar disorder are also known as manic episodes, and the extreme lows are called depressive episodes.

During depressive disorders, a person's autobiographic memory network is stuck being turned on. This means that the person is forced to think far too much about themselves, which can come in the form of self-loathing, brooding, or ruminating.

Simultaneously, there is a suppression of the cognitive control network, resulting in the manifestation of symptoms such as diminished concentration, reduced cognitive processing speed, and impaired decision-making abilities in the individual.

The primary therapeutic interventions for depressive disorders encompass transcranial magnetic stimulation (TMS), a technique that involves the targeted activation of the cognitive control network to enhance its functionality. Various pharmaceutical interventions can also be employed to reinstate the equilibrium of the body's neurochemicals, hence facilitating the interplay between the aforementioned networks and the limbic system.

Numerous therapeutic interventions exist with the objective of empowering individuals experiencing distress, facilitating their ability to regain mastery over their emotional state. Psychologists commonly instruct their patients to use their cognitive control network during training sessions. One approach to achieving this objective involves encouraging patients to engage in cognitive restructuring, when they actively confront their negative thoughts in order to enhance their capacity for rational thinking. The implementation of mindfulness techniques can potentially disrupt an individual's autobiographical memory network, hence challenging their dominant cognitive processes.

Despite the brain comprising various processes that are crucial to the processing of emotions and behaviours, ongoing research is currently dedicated to exploring the intricate relationship between the brain and emotions.

The ABC Model is a theoretical framework commonly used in psychology and cognitive-behavioural therapy to understand the relationship between thoughts, emotions, and behaviours. It posits that

One significant facet of social anxiety entails the process of ruminating over one's behaviour subsequent to a social event. It is customary to engage in introspection and evaluate one's social demeanour and impact on others. However, excessive rumination and the tendency to excessively scrutinise one's actions are unproductive and offer no benefits to individuals involved. This methodology facilitates the comprehension of how our personal views can contribute to suboptimal outcomes in social contexts. This approach comprises three components.

The letter "A" refers to the term "antecedent." This event serves as the catalyst for the cognitive processes and actions that necessitate comprehension.

One aspect that plays a significant role in shaping individuals' perspectives and actions is their beliefs. Upon the identification of the preceding occurrence, the subsequent step involves the identification of the associated beliefs. As an illustration, one might have had the belief that they would experience embarrassment during the course of this particular incident. Alternatively, one may have made the decision that no one encountered at the event would exhibit a strong alignment with one's own values or beliefs. Certain beliefs may be readily apparent, while others may reside in the realm of the subconscious. It is crucial to ascertain these ideas in order to comprehend their influence on our behaviours in specific circumstances.

The letter "C" represents the concept of consequence. Presently, our focus lies on the examination of our conduct during these occurrences and the subsequent influence it exerts on our engagements inside social contexts.

By engaging in the process outlined, we will gain insight into the manner in which our personal convictions shape the world we perceive. This approach will facilitate the assumption of responsibility for our actions before to, during, and subsequent to social interactions.

The concept of SMART goal-setting is a well recognised and effective approach in various fields, including education, business, and personal development.

This methodology centres on modifying our behaviours with a specific objective in mind. In the context of social anxiety, individuals often want to ameliorate their symptoms and establish meaningful connections with others. Nevertheless, there is a lack of clarity regarding the initial steps to be undertaken and the precise course of action to be pursued. The acronym SMART represents the following components of effective goal-setting: ● definite: Goals should be clearly defined and focused. ● Measurable: Goals should be quantifiable and capable of being assessed. ● Achievable: Goals should be attainable and within one's capabilities. ● Realistic: Goals should be practical and feasible given the available resources. ● Time-bound: Goals should have a definite timeframe or deadline for completion.

Let us endeavour to comprehend this strategy through the utilisation of an illustrative instance. The individual expresses a desire to increase their level of vocal participation within their workplace, although they are uncertain about the appropriate means by which to achieve this objective. It is possible to establish goals in collaboration with one's therapist. The proposed objective is dedicating one hour during lunchtime on a weekly basis to engage in conversations with either a fellow coworker or a mentor. I shall accomplish this objective by extending an invitation to partake in a shared meal with them. The objective at hand is to commence the process of engaging in dialogues with one's colleagues in the workplace. In this context, the individual is required to undertake a designated duty involving the act of extending an invitation to an individual to partake in a midday meal on a weekly basis, with the duration of the engagement being limited to one hour. This objective is readily quantifiable and achievable. Is it feasible within the realm of practicality? Consider the manner in which individuals within a professional setting engage in social interactions during the designated midday break. Is there a prevailing culture inside your office characterised by a tendency for individuals to exhibit warmth and friendliness? Have you ever received invitations to socialise with others and opted to decline them in the past? If affirmative, it is highly probable that individuals would derive pleasure from engaging in leisurely activities in your company. Additionally, it is possible to establish a predetermined timeframe for the attainment of this objective. For instance, one may opt to engage in this particular exercise for a duration of three months, thereby enabling the systematic monitoring of personal advancement throughout this period. During this temporal period, it is advisable to document one's emotional state prior to extending an invitation for a lunch engagement, during the ensuing talk, and subsequent to the interaction.

Does one's level of confidence tend to increase over time? Is there a mutual exchange of laughter or engaging discourse with another individual? Are you aware of the substantial similarities that exist between yourself and another individual? It is quite probable that one's interpersonal exchanges will surpass initial expectations, and even those encounters that do not unfold favourably would likely be less unfavourable than initially perceived. In alternative terms, it is probable that you will possess a more impartial understanding of your abilities as a communicator.

There are several ailments in which the exacerbation of symptoms can be attributed to stress. These disorders include cardiovascular problems, asthma, multiple sclerosis, chronic pain, acne, fibromyalgia, and depression.

Although stress itself is not considered a direct cause of cardiovascular disease or high blood pressure, it has the potential to exacerbate the progression of these conditions in certain individuals.

The immune system is also impacted by stress.

Several studies have indicated that acute, short-term stressors have the potential to enhance the immunological response of the human body. However, it has been observed that chronic, long-term stress has the adverse effect of gradually weakening the immune system, hence increasing susceptibility to common colds and other diseases.

Empirical research has additionally demonstrated that stress might potentially diminish the immune response to immunisations and impede the process of wound healing.

Strategies for effectively managing stress in a health-conscious manner

Stress is typically associated with a combination of external and internal factors.

External components encompass several aspects of an individual's life, such as the physical environment, occupational engagements, interpersonal interactions, residential circumstances, as well as the diverse array of situations, challenges, complexities, and anticipations encountered on a day-to-day basis.

The internal factors of an individual have an impact on their physiological ability to respond to and manage external stressors.

The internal factors that influence an individual's ability to effectively cope with stress encompass their dietary status, overall physical health and fitness, emotional state, capability to control stress through relaxation techniques or other strategies, and the amount of sleep and rest they obtain.

The management of stress entails acquiring strategies to enhance both external factors that one encounters and internal factors that contribute to one's ability to effectively cope with challenges.

There are five fundamental strategies that can potentially aid in reducing stress.

The following strategies can be employed to enhance well-being and productivity: 1. Physical Activity: Engaging in regular exercise has been shown to have numerous benefits for both physical and mental health. 2. Relaxation and Meditation Techniques: Incorporating relaxation and meditation practises into one's routine can help reduce stress and promote a sense of calm and well-being. 3. Effective Time Management: Developing effective time management skills can aid in prioritising tasks, incre

What are the potential ways in which exercise can aid in the management of stress?

Physical activity: Engaging in physical activity has been found to have potential benefits in terms of relaxation and sleep promotion.

Physical activity can potentially serve as a prominent and fundamental approach to cope with stress.

Engaging in physical exercise not only contributes to overall physical well-being, but also serves as a means to effectively manage mental tension and worry.

Physical activity can also contribute to relaxation and the facilitation of sleep.

Conclusion

The individual's pursuit to conquer social anxiety has been characterized by bravery and significant personal growth. In this book, the reader has examined the intricacies of social anxiety, acquired knowledge regarding its origins and consequences, and uncovered a variety of approaches and methods to regain autonomy and flourish in social contexts. Upon arriving at this conclusion, it is imperative to engage in introspection over one's progress and duly recognize the noteworthy advancements that have been achieved.

The Act of Commemorating Personal Accomplishments:

It is important to pause and acknowledge one's accomplishments, regardless of their magnitude. The progression of your actions, the obstacles encountered, and the accomplishments achieved have together contributed to the development of your own growth and fortitude.

Reflecting on the Expedition:

Reflect upon instances in which the experience of social anxiety was particularly intense and seemingly insurmountable. Acknowledge the significant progress that has been made since that time and reflect upon the substantial self-discovery that has been achieved during the journey.

Advancing Your Journey towards Expansion:

While embarking on your expedition, it is imperative to bear in mind the following principles:

The concept of self-compassion refers to the practice of treating oneself with kindness, understanding It is advisable to exhibit kindness and patience towards oneself. Self-compassion serves as the fundamental basis for enduring transformation.

Persistence is a crucial factor in comprehending that the process of conquering social anxiety is continuous and requires consistent effort. Adversities are a common occurrence, and each one presents a potential for personal development.

Maintaining and nurturing one's support network is crucial for fostering interpersonal connections. Maintain regular communication with individuals or social networks, such as friends, family members, or support groups, that have played a significant role in facilitating your personal development.

Embracing Novel Opportunities: A Willingness to Engage with New Ventures and Obstacles. Continuously strive to broaden your comfort zone, and refrain from hesitating to engage in novel experiences or assume unfamiliar responsibilities.

Professional Support: In the event that it is necessary, it is advisable to persist in the pursuit of professional assistance. Therapists and counselors possess the capacity to provide individuals with vital insights, coping mechanisms, and a secure environment for the purpose of self-expression.

The concept of lifelong learning entails acknowledging that personal development is an ongoing process that spans across one's entire lifespan. It is imperative to persist in the pursuit of novel methodologies, cultivate aptitudes, and enhance one's approaches.

The Concept of Authentic Living: The ultimate objective is to lead an authentic life that is congruent with one's values and objectives. Persevere in your pursuit of a life characterized by self-assurance, satisfaction, and significant interpersonal relationships.

One's identity is not determined by social anxiety; instead, it represents a formidable obstacle that has been bravely confronted and is being overcome. Through the cultivation of persistence, self-compassion, and an unrelenting dedication to personal development, individuals has the capacity to mold a forthcoming trajectory characterized by a profound sense of self-assurance, meaningful interpersonal relationships, and boundless opportunities. The ongoing progression of your path propels you towards the attainment of a flourishing and genuine existence that is rightfully yours.

www.ingramcontent.com/pod-product-compliance
Lightning Source LLC
Chambersburg PA
CBHW052143110526
44591CB00012B/1831